LIVING AND NONLIVING

Prairie

Cassie Mayer

Heinemann Library
Chicago, Illinois

Photo research by Tracy Cummins
Designed by Kimberly Miracle
Printed and bound in the United States of America in Eau Claire, Wisconsin.   042013   007338RP
15 14 13
10 9 8 7 6 5 4 3

Library of Congress Cataloging-in-Publication Data
Mayer, Cassie.
  Prairie / Cassie Mayer.
    p. cm. -- (Living and nonliving)
  Includes bibliographical references and index.
  ISBN-13: 978-1-4034-9428-3 (hc)
  ISBN-13: 978-1-4034-9434-4 (pb)
 1. Prairie ecology--Juvenile literature. 2. Prairies--Juvenile literature. I. Title.
  QH541.5.P7M39 2007
  577.4'4--dc22
                       2006037976

Acknowledgements
The author and publisher are grateful to the following for the permission to reproduce copyright material:
Alamy pp. **16** (Creatas/Dynamic Graphics Group), **19** (Jaubert Bernard), **23** (river: Creatas/Dynamic Graphics Group); Ardea p. **10** (Chris Knights); Corbis pp. **7** (W. Perry Conway), **8** (D. Robert & Lorri Franz), **9** (W. Perry Conway), **14** (Macduff Everton), **15** (Richard T. Nowitz), **17** (Visions of America/ Joseph Sohm); Getty Images pp. **4** (Stone/Frank Oberle), **5** (Stone/Frank Oberle), **6** (National Geographic/Klaus Nigge), **13** (Stone/ Jake Rajs), **21** (Stone/Frank Oberle), **23** (bison: Stone/Jake Rajs; prairie: Stone/Frank Oberle); Masterfile p. **18** (Daryl Benson); Natural Visions p. **11** (Heather Angel); Nature Picture Library pp. **12** (Pete Cairns), **20** (Larry Michael); Photolibrary p. **22** (The Travel Library Limited).

Cover photograph reproduced with permission of Getty Images/The Image Bank/Terry Donnelly. Back cover photograph reproduced with permission of Alamy/Creatas/Dynamic Graphics Group.

Every effort has been made to contact copyright holders of any material reproduces in this book.
Any omissions will be rectified in subsequent printings if notice is given to the publisher.

Contents

A Prairie Habitat

A prairie is an open area of land.
A prairie does not have many trees.

A prairie has living things.
A prairie has nonliving things.

Owl in the Prairie

burrowing owl

Is an owl living?

Does an owl need food? *Yes.*
Does an owl need water? *Yes.*

Does an owl need air? *Yes.*

Does an owl grow? *Yes.*

An owl is living.

Bison in the Prairie

Is a bison living?

Does a bison need food? *Yes.*
Does a bison need water? *Yes.*

Does a bison need air? *Yes.*

Does a bison grow? *Yes.*

A bison is living.

River in the Prairie

Is a river living?

Does a river need food? *No.*
Does a river need more water? *No.*

Does a river need air? *No.*

Does a river grow? *No.*

A river is not living.

Grass in the Prairie

Is grass living?

Does grass need food? *Yes.*
Does grass need water? *Yes.*

Does grass need air? *Yes.*

Does grass grow? *Yes.*

Grass is living.

A prairie is home to many things.
A prairie is an important habitat.

Picture Glossary

 **habitat** an area where plants and animals live

 **prairie** a habitat that has flat land and few trees

 **river** a small body of water

Index

Note to Parents and Teachers
Each book in this series uses patterned question-and-answer text to identify the basic characteristics of living things. Discuss with students other familiar living and nonliving things and ask them to think of additional criteria that would help classify an object as living or nonliving.

The text has been chosen with the advice of a literacy expert to enable beginning readers success in reading independently or with moderate support. An expert was consulted to ensure accurate content. You can support children's nonfiction literacy skills by helping them use the table of contents, headings, picture glossary, and index.